THE MOON

For Kids

Copyright © 2024 Samuel John

THE MOON

Before we begin, we must be very clear about one thing...

What is the Moon?

The Moon is a natural satellite.

And what is a satellite? A satellite is a celestial object that orbits around a planet. That is, it circles around it.

The Moon rotates around the Earth and is the only natural satellite of our planet. However, there are hundreds of natural satellites in our solar system.

THE MOVEMENTS OF THE MOON

The Moon is always on the move - it never stands still!

Did you know that the Moon takes 28 days to complete one revolution around the Earth?

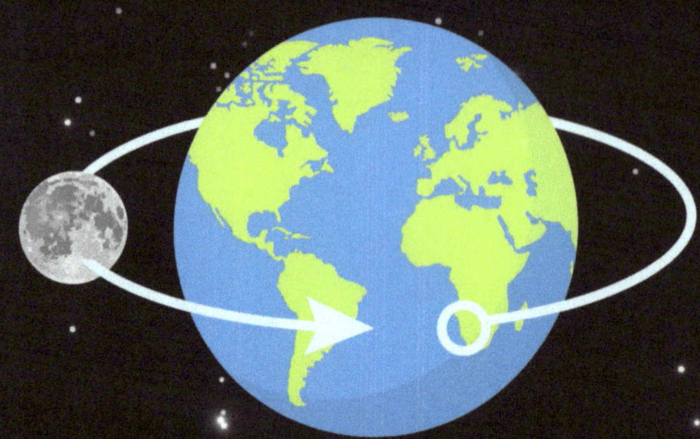

But that's not all! The Moon also performs another movement: rotation. In this motion, the Moon spins around on itself, like a spinning top or like a ballerina that spins around without moving from the same place. And guess what, this motion also takes 28 days to complete! Isn't it amazing?

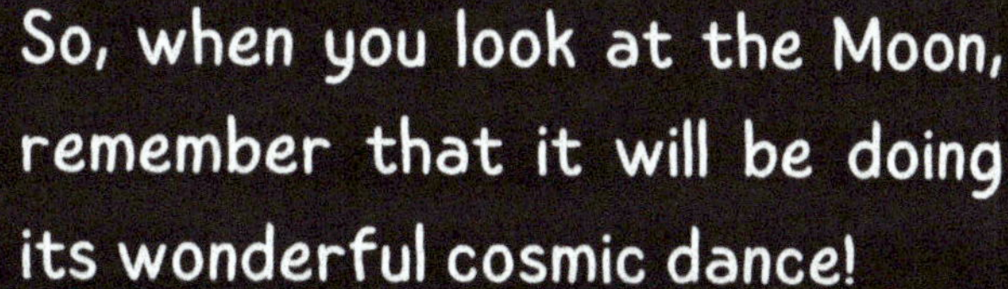

THE TWO FACES OF THE MOON

Have you ever wondered why we always see the same face of the Moon?

That's because it takes the same amount of time to go around its axis as it takes to go around the Earth.

Imagine you are in the center of a room and a friend is standing three paces away facing you. Then, your friend moves in a circle around the room, looking at you. That's what happens with the Moon and the Earth!

While the Moon has a face that is always visible, it also has a mysterious hidden face that we never see from Earth.

THE SHAPES OF THE MOON

Why does the Moon change its appearance in the sky? Let's discover the mystery of the moon phases!

If we observe the moon for several days, we will notice that it changes shape. These changes are known as lunar phases and are repeated every 28 days.

The first thing you should know is that the Moon has no light of its own. So why do we see it shining at night? This is because there is a mirror effect. The light from the Sun reflects off the Moon and that's why we see it illuminated in the sky.

During its journey around the Earth, the Moon receives more or less light from the Sun, depending on its position. This is what makes us see the Moon differently every night!

Don't worry, you'll understand it better below...

NEW MOON

In this phase, the Moon is located between the Earth and the Sun.

Its illuminated side points towards the Sun and its dark side towards the Earth.

For this reason, the Moon is hardly visible in the sky, or, in some cases, we cannot see it at all.

WAXING CRESCENT

This phase occurs approximately one week after the New Moon.

At this stage, part of the illuminated side of the Moon faces the Earth.

It is called "crescent" because the illuminated part we see is getting larger and larger.

It occurs approximately one week after the waxing crescent.

In this phase, the Earth is located between the Moon and the Sun.

This means that we can see the entire illuminated part of the Moon in the sky. It looks "full", complete.

WANING CRESCENT

During this phase of the Moon, we see the opposite half of the illuminated side that we saw during the waxing crescent.

It is called "waning" because the illuminated part becomes smaller and smaller.

WAXING CRESCENT OR WANING CRESCENT?

A simple trick to find out whether the Moon is in the waxing or waning phase is this:

- When the Moon is in the waxing crescent phase, it is in the shape of a "D".
- When it is in the waning crescent phase, the Moon is in the shape of a "C"

- "C" shape
- It is decreasing
- Waning Crescent

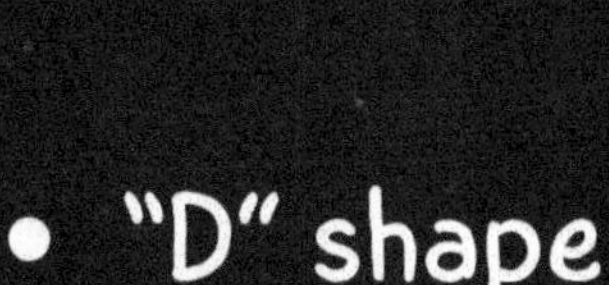

- "D" shape
- Is growing
- Waxing Crescent

So, a Moon in the Waning Crescent will have its left side visible and in the Waxing Crescent, we will see its right side illuminated.

THE MOON MOVES AWAY FROM THE EARTH

The average distance between the Earth and the Moon is 384,400 km (238 855 miles), but...

Did you know that the Moon is moving away from the Earth by almost 3.82 cm per year (1.5 inches)?

This means that, a long time ago, the Moon was closer to the Earth and in the future, we will see it further away from us.

In the past

In the future

THE MOON LANDING

On 20 July 1969, the astronauts of the Apollo 11 mission landed on the Moon.

Commander Neil Armstrong became the first human to walk on the moon, followed by pilot Buzz Aldrin.

They collected rock samples, put up a flag and returned as heroes.

It was a very exciting moment and the whole planet was following the event.

GRAVITY ON THE MOON

Gravity is like a powerful magnet that keeps us attracted to the ground. When you throw something up in the air, gravity is what makes it quickly return to the ground.

On Earth, that "magnet" is very strong, but on the Moon, it is weaker.

If you were on the Moon, you would weigh less!

> The weight of an object on the Moon is about six times less than on Earth.

For example: if you weigh 30 kg (66 lb) on Earth, on the Moon you would weigh about 5 kg (11 lb).

30 kg (66 lb)   5 kg (11 lb)

THE CRATERS OF THE MOON

Craters on the Moon are holes formed on its surface by the impact of asteroids and meteorites.

The Moon has thousands of them, due to all the impacts it has suffered over millions of years.

So, craters are like scars on the Moon.

Every time you look at the Moon, think of these craters as part of its incredible adventure in space!

And here it ends!

I hope you liked it and learned new things.

Until next time!

I want to ask you a favor so that this book reaches more people, and that is that you rate it with a sincere opinion on the platform where you purchased it.

With that small gesture, you will be helping me to carry on with new projects.

I can't wait to start creating my next book for you!

You can leave your review directly here. It will only take you a few seconds.

www.amzn.to/4by51J2

Thank you in advance for taking time to share your experience. I appreciate your support!

See you soon!

LEARN WITH OUR
EDUCATIONAL CHILDREN'S BOOKS

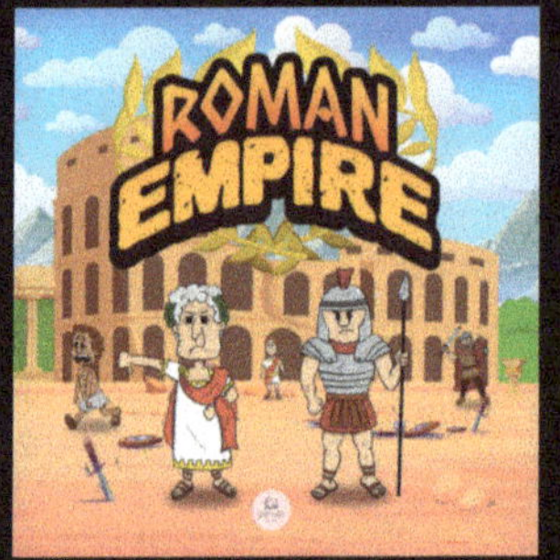

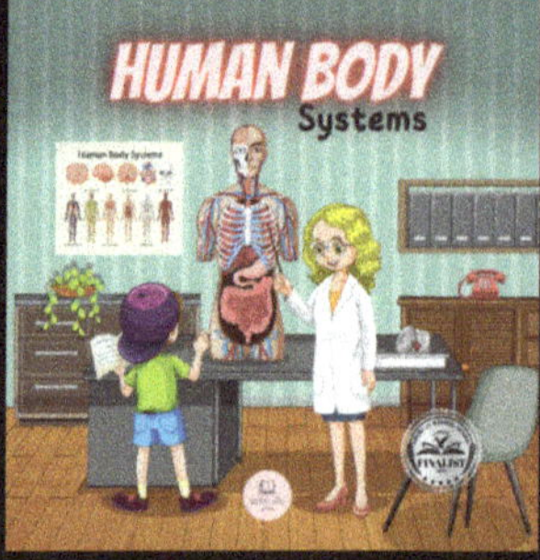

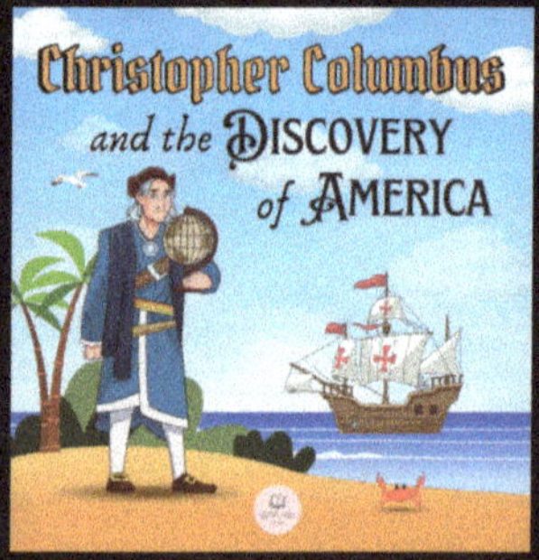

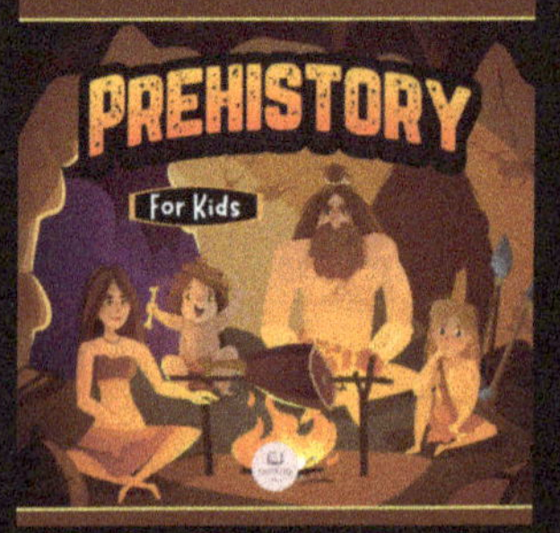

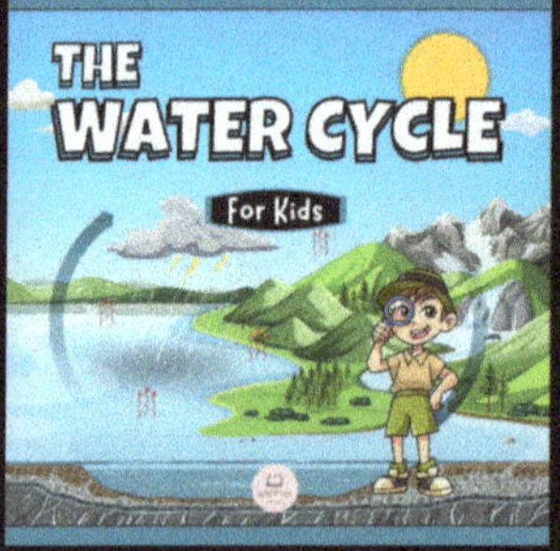

https://www.pge.me/childrensbooks

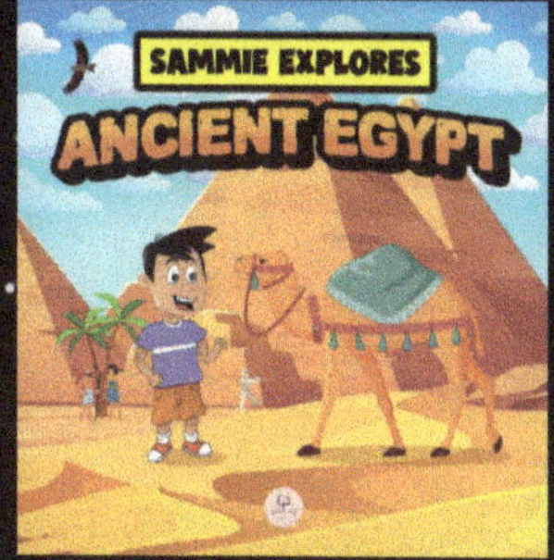

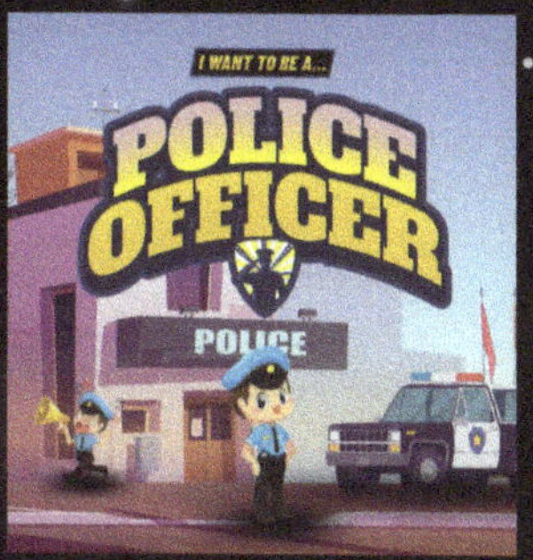

Do you have any ideas for a new educational book? I love hearing the thoughts and suggestions from my young readers!

If there's a topic you'd like to see covered in an upcoming book, let me know! Reach out to me via email, and I'll consider your suggestion. Remember, it should be an educational topic!

 **contacto@samueljohnbooks.com**

This book comes to life with downloadable audio. Perfect for engaging young readers and sparking their imagination.

www.bit.ly/TheMoonAudio